SHOUTING DOWN THE SILENCE

Books By Morton Marcus

Origins (Kayak, 1969)
Where The Oceans Cover Us (Capra, 1972)
The Santa Cruz Mountain Poems (Capra, 1972)
The Armies Encamped In The Fields Beyond The Unfinished Avenues: Prose Poems (Jazz Press, 1977)
Big Winds, Glass Mornings, Shadows Cast By Stars: Poems, 1972-1980 (Jazz Press, 1980)
The Brezhnev Memo (Dell/Delacorte, 1981) {Novel}
Pages From A Scrapbook Of Immigrants (Coffee House, 1988)
When People Could Fly: Prose Poems (Hanging Loose, 1997)
Moments Without Names: New and Selected Prose Poems (White Pine Press, 2002)

SHOUTING DOWN THE SILENCE

Verse Poems, 1988-2001

MORTON MARCUS

A DONALD S. ELLIS BOOK

CREATIVE ARTS BOOK COMPANY
Berkeley • California

Copyright © 2002 by Morton Marcus

No part of this book may be reproduced in any manner
without written permission from the publisher,
except in brief quotations used in articles and reviews.

Shouting Down the Silence
is published by Donald S. Ellis
and distributed by Creative Arts Book Company

For information contact:
Creative Arts Book Company
833 Bancroft Way
Berkeley, California 94710
1-800-848-7789

The cover illustration, "The Smoker" by Georges de La Tour,
is from the collection of The Tokyo Fuji Art Museum,
and is used by permission of the museum.

Library of Congress Cataloging-in-Publication Data

Marcus, Morton.
    Shouting down the silence: verse poems, 1988-2001 / Morton Marcus.
       p. cm.
    "A Donald S. Ellis book."
    ISBN 0-88739 453-1 (alk. paper)
      I. Title.
    PS3563.A639 S56 2002
    811'.54--dc21
                                                   2002019693

Printed in the United States of America

Acknowledgements

Grateful acknowledgement is made to the following publications where many of these poems originally appeared, some of them in slightly different forms:

The Alembic: "Quartet In A Minor Key"
The Antioch Review: "Chekhov's Funeral"
The Barnabe Mt. Review: "My Daughters Grown," "I Have A Talk With My Right Foot," "Sculptors"
The Bellingham Review: "After The End" (as "Penelope" and "Odysseus")
The Bloomsbury Review: "Shouting Down The Silence"
The Cafe Review: "The Tooth Fairy," "Where Do The Shadows Go"
Chelsea: "Rabelais, 1553"
Durak: "Sub-Division"
Dryad: "Such Friends"
Hanging Loose: "Waking," "Balzac," "The Blessing," "That Morning"
Homestead Review: "Dawn"
Luna: "The Other," "The Poem About Light"
Ploughshares: "My Aloneness," "Our Star," "Haydn, 1772"
Poetry International: "A Triptych For Giacometti"
Portland Review: "Clear Night"
Real World Press: "Year After Year"
Red Dirt: "Looking For Vasko Popa"
Red Wheelbarrow: "A Letter (1885)," "Suffering," "Rodin & Rilke: Meudon, 1902"

In addition, several of these pieces first appeared in the anthologies:

A Gathering of Poets (Kent State Press): "The Cell"
The Last Dance (Mayfield): "Luka Stanoš"
Small Town Roadstops (Portofino Café): "My Aloneness"
New American Poets of The '80s (Wampeter): "Tongue"
The Geography of Home (Hey Day): "The Poem For Gonzales, California"
Chinatown Dreams: The Photographs of George Lee (Capitola Book Company):
        "The Chinese Immigrant's Lament"

for my family

Rae
Donna
Jana
Valerie
and Nick

This earth will grow cold one day,
not like a heap of ice
or a dead cloud even,
but like an empty walnut it will roll along
        in pitch-black space…
You must grieve for this right now,
you have to feel this sorrow now,
for the world must be loved this much
        if you're going to say "I lived"…

— *Nazim Hikmet*

CONTENTS

1. Lost Homes

My Aloneness.... 1
The Tooth Fairy.... 2
Totem.... 5
That Morning.... 7
Waking.... 11
Such Friends.... 13
The Poem For Gonzales, California.... 14
My Daughters Grown.... 16
Sub-Division.... 18
M & Ms.... 19
Our Star.... 22
Roses.... 24

2. Foreign Places

The Old Country.... 31
Dawn.... 32
Majke Jevrosime #3.... 33
Luka Stanoš.... 37
Looking For Vasko Popa.... 40
St. Mark's Cathedral.... 43
Letter To Czeslaw Milosz.... 47
The Boy in the Painting.... 49
The Chinese Immigrant's Lament.... 50
After The End.... 52
"Once I Woke".... 54
Year After Year.... 55

3. The Glorious Dead

Rabelais, 1553.... 61
Haydn, 1772.... 62
Shelley's Funeral.... 63
Balzac, 1850.... 64
Quartet In A Minor Key.... 65
A Letter (1885).... 68
Chekhov's Funeral.... 70
Rodin & Rilke.... 71
The Blessing.... 73
Celine.... 74
A Triptych For Giacometti.... 75
Suffering.... 77

4. Shouting Down The Silence

Tongue.... 83
The Cell.... 84
The Other.... 88
I Have A Talk With My Right Foot.... 90
Where Do The Shadows Go.... 92
Sculptors.... 94
The Poem About Light.... 96
Old Men, Old Women.... 99
Clear Night.... 101
The Stars.... 102
No Matter What.... 103
Shouting Down The Silence.... 104

SHOUTING DOWN THE SILENCE

1

LOST HOMES

MY ALONENESS

Nights standing in a field
or sleeping under the stars,
I sense that one of those pebbles of light
is signalling me from deep space.
I know this is nothing more
than my own longing cast like fishing line
into the depths of another kind of ocean,
and that my aloneness
is reflected in whatever rock chip
I can imagine out there,
but there's a comfort I won't deny
in the images and word groupings
I invent, no matter how outlandish
or ornate they are, or bare.
And when I realize that nothing
is going to respond to my bait,
and that I'm standing at the edge
of a bustling milky stream
packed with sparkling shards
of dumb rock, there's something
terrifying yet wonderful
about acknowledging
my complete aloneness
that only this procedure can impart,
like standing one foggy dawn
ankle-deep in a freezing brook
with no one else around
just as the sun burns through
and the trees like tattered thoughts
release the hidden circle of the sky—
endless, empty, cold, and blue.

THE TOOTH FAIRY

1.

We never even caught
a glimpse of her, the one
who took our teeth and left
a quarter beneath the pillow
as a reward for growing up.
I wanted to see her,
the Tooth Fairy:
I wanted to see her naked,
her porcelain body
as cold and gleaming
as Dresden china.
If I put a bright new coin
beneath my pillow,
I thought, its light
would so surprise her
I could catch her wrists
and hold her past that moment
when the earth turned
beyond her timetable,
or whatever coordinates
allowed her to travel
between her world and ours.
But if I caught her,
would she shatter
in my arms? Would
she become a gown
tumbling like a waterfall
into a puddle at my feet?
Once I thought I had her,
but she escaped
disguised as a shudder,
and I woke with my arms
hugging my naked chest
as if I was clinging
to an exhaled breath.

2.

And I wanted to go there,
where the Tooth Fairy
kept her treasure.
I wanted to go to that
moon-enamelled mountain
rising from the snow
like an incisor jutting
from the discarded jawbone
of a giant. Each night
the Tooth Fairy
flew to a cave high
on the slopes of that
tooth-shaped mountain
where she emptied her sack
of fresh teeth. They echoed
through ice-glazed caverns,
clattering against the teeth
she had scattered
in those tunnels before,
as if the mountain
was a depository of skulls
from the beginning of time,
grains of sand pouring through
a porcelain hourglass. That
was the Tooth Fairy's treasure,
and the moon shone down
on our world and hers like a coin
that hung in the sky
as a reminder of payment,
a payment my grandfather
and my father had made
when their heads on the pillow
were gone one morning,
never to return.

3.

That was why I wanted
to catch the Tooth Fairy
and hold her fast.
"Give me back my father,"
I'd say as she fought
to get loose. "Give me
my grandparents,"
and I'd clutch her close.

I haven't forgotten
the Tooth Fairy,
and still grab at anything
she might be—clothes
capering on a washline,
shadows sliding down a wall.
But now no coins appear
to reward me for the teeth
that drop from my jaw
or are wrenched
from my face. My heart,
a toothless mouth
that keeps gorging
like a frog in my chest,
is no prince, and my lungs
no wings to fly me
past the moon that slides
above my nights
like a silver lure
trolling the black pond
in which I sleep.

TOTEM

As a boy, I always thought
that insects were so well bred:
the fly thoroughly washing
his whole head, or scrubbing
his back feet; the spider
embroidering doorways and corners
with doilies worthy to grace
the fussiest old lady's home.
It was encouraging to see
how our health habits
and refined tastes were being
practiced in the animal world.
It let me know that God
was seated above the planet
on a golden throne, draped
in a billowing white robe
composed of all the dead—
those who had lived
and those who had not:
God was all dressed up in souls,
overseeing his universe,
each moment directing
a soul to depart like fuzz
he flicked from the arm
of his robe, a sunbeam
that spun toward the Earth
with millions of others,
passing those gray beams
drifting upward toward His throne.

Why was it, then, I always turned
and thought of bear, that great padder
who slept all winter in a cave
but rose each evening,
his fur mashed with piss-stench
and berry-shit, to thud
one uncertain foot after another
into the snow. Barely balancing

his ponderous weight, he plodded
over logs and cold stones,
his small, angry eyes
intent on what was ahead,
as he grunted and lunged forward,
lumbering through frozen meadows
on his way to my home.
Every night I heard him
trudging up the stairs
to my bedroom door
where he waited until morning,
shifting from foot to foot,
snuffling, coughing behind a paw.
He waits there now, more
a jealous but protective brother
than an avenging angel,
and more a father than a god.

THAT MORNING

I start out on the page
as I did that morning,
leaving the lobby
and its glass door
encased in black grille work,
scraping my sneakers
on the sidewalk past
the bus stop and newstand,
and prancing by the park
on the small island
in the middle of traffic,
the one with the statue
of the Liberator astride
the rearing bronze horse,
pointing his sword
toward Liberty or Destiny.
In the same way, I write
my way down this page,
describing a morning
forgotten in childhood
to make of it something
more than description, not
remembering where
I was headed or whether
it was Brooklyn or Vilna,
or if I am the one strutting
through the traffic, or if
it is my grandfather
strolling to work years before
and about to encounter
the old woman who would
change his life forever.
Or maybe it's both of us
in my body as I make my way
to school two blocks over,
the warm apartment
receding behind me,
the sunlight pale as the beer

I hadn't tasted yet, not
at that age, but want to use
as an image here to mark
the moment the old woman
I hadn't noticed hobbled
into my consciousness.
She was there, in my path,
smiling and reaching out,
just as my friend Freddie
shouted behind me,
"Hey, Mort, wait up,"
and turned the day away
from the old woman
who, having stopped,
was about to say something
that may have changed
my life forever. "Help me,"
she may have said, and fallen.
 Or "Do you know Harold
Dubin?. . . I've come so far. . ."
But it was Freddie with
a fistful of baseball cards
I turned to, spared for a time
an intrusion from beyond
the neighborhood. I think
she must have watched us
drag our satchels and say words
like "DiMaggio" and "Williams,"
not understanding, thinking
we spoke another language.
Maybe she held a slip of paper
toward me when she said,
"I've come so far. . ."
Did she really say that,
or did it happen on this page
because I want it to now,
so I can go back and change
my life from that point,
saying something like,
"Yes, I know Harold Dubin,"
although I wouldn't know him

until boot camp years later,
where we prepared for a war
he wouldn't return from.
If I had told the old woman
I knew him, when I met
Harold Dubin that first time
in the barracks, I could have said,
"One morning when I was a kid,
there was this old woman
who was looking for you.
She'd come a long way,"
and maybe his life would
have changed somehow.
Instead, I said, "I lived there too,
until I was twelve, three years
before DiMaggio retired. I
remember how the sunlight
was pale as beer there
in the morning. Strange."
The day I saw the old woman,
there was a war somewhere,
or there was about to be one,
the one that would kill Harold
Dubin, not the one that might
have killed us all, herding us
behind barbed wire—mothers,
sisters, dads, whole families—
where smokestacks pointed
like cannon toward heaven.
If I had been caught in that one,
the words on this page
would not have been written,
nor would the old woman
have come so far, hobbling
past me with her slip of paper
like a pale flame leading her
toward someone who had died
too young, if that phrase means
anything. Maybe she had come
to warn him, and if I had told her
he lived two buildings down,

I would have changed his life.
Or was she the one looking
for my grandfather in Vilna
all those years ago in the story
he used to tell about the old lady
who had stopped him in the street
to deliver the letter with the tickets
that had changed his life forever.
That event, he always added,
had occurred under the statue
of the Liberator and his horse
riding into a battle of great import
with a name like Liberty
or Destiny. By this he implied
that his emigration was destined
and his journey a mythical battle,
clearly not to be confused
with the battle most of us fight
each day to keep going,
as we try to make more of our days
than just the salary or the tedium
of the job behind the counter
or on the assembly line. Ours
is the battle Harold Dubin
never fought or worked at,
or would have died to protect,
but it is an extension of both
my grandfather's journey
and Harold Dubin's war,
and may well have been the impulse
that drove me to write this page,
trying to make something more
than description about a morning
that may never have happened
and certainly wasn't pale as beer
but that if I describe it that way
and get the description right
just may change your life,
or somebody else's, forever.

WAKING

Once I woke on a picnic table
by the side of a highway in Illinois,
next to a girl whose name I couldn't remember.
Her odor was all over me
and mine all over her.

I was twenty, and still drunk,
and what had wakened me was the dawn,
a bloodshot eye emerging from layers of mist
like the anger of God rising in my face.
I snickered. "The hell you say," I said aloud to the sky,
knowing how the mind makes of the world
whatever it wants to. I didn't even wake the girl.

The days go over my head like dusty herds,
but that dawn rises in my brain again and again.
The stop was in a clump of trees I'd pass
driving to and from the base,
and for the next year I'd think of her.
I've never been back: it was just a roadside stop—
tables, benches, two garbage cans—
memorable for nothing, except that dawn.

At twenty I expected so much from the days
that came at me as I went face forward into them:
I wanted to be a man and hoped someone,
tall and proud, would happen along
and show me how it was done,
and somehow I'd know,
somehow I'd walk differently
and be a person I could be proud of.

She was twenty-three. We never said goodbye.
And I never took her number.
Not that it would have made a difference.

Once it was "the hell you say"
and squirting spit between my teeth,

while voices spoke from the other side of thunder
and I refused to listen. Now it is these words
that have nothing more to tell me.

                           As for the girl,
she went away into the afternoon,
other nights, other dawns, other men,
until, I'd like to think, she found someone
who would wake her, or who she would wake,
when either of them heard the other
muttering in the dark.

SUCH FRIENDS

Drunk on ale from green quart bottles,
my friend, a young poet, weeps,
thinking of my wife alone on the hill.
His woman, ironing in the other room,
weeps too, remembering how she was left,
husband and friend gone on a night like this
never to return. Even the dead old poet Roethke's
Belgian bargehound is morose, and waddles up
to nudge me with his nose and stare so forlornly
I think the poet has risen in him
to show me through his eyes
a knowledge I won't accept.

                        So much grief:
each house sends up a baying to the moon.
All lives are broken in the end,
and their sorrows rise like smoke
from countless chimneys,
only to flood back down again
like moonlight through the windows.

I am moved by a sadness here
that is like no other:
a man, a woman, and a poet's ghost
weeping for a sorrow not their own.
They suffer for my wife,
who sits alone in a moonlit house
and does not know her grief
has touched their lives.

                        When the time comes,
may such friends weep for me.

THE POEM FOR GONZALES, CALIFORNIA

for Tony Doyle

Gonzales will always be
a cold, clear night
in early March, a place
on Highway 101
between Soledad and Salinas
where, returning late
from a trip to Santa Barbara,
I chose to pull off the road
and drive into a field,
exhausted, sick in soul,
halfway to divorce and as sure
of my own death as I was
of the sour milk taste
coating the inside of my mouth.
When I switched off the engine
I heard the breathing
of my two small daughters
asleep in the back seat,
and knew that they would
continue on without me,
that the world would,
with no fanfare and less
concern.

       A deep quiet
settled around the car.
The dark field encircled me.
The stars, a glittering panorama
through the windshield, ticked
across the sky. I was more alone
than I had ever been,
and didn't know
where that realization
would lead me.

                Shut in that car—
an insect in his carapace
surrounded by the field
and the endless, inching
movement of the stars—
I listened to the breathing
from the back seat, knowing
that whatever I decided
would determine
the rest of my life.
Ten minutes later
I flipped on the ignition
and drove toward home.

                          This happened
in Gonzales, California,
a town that a friend now tells me
has been taken off the map.
It happened in a field
I could never find again
but have marked on my memory
as the place at my back
I start from and continue on.

MY DAUGHTERS GROWN

1.

I have returned numberless times
to that room where my daughters slept
when they were seven and two
and I heard the slender wings
of their breathing climb
and hover above their heads,
a slow flexing in that house
they haven't lived in for twenty years.

It is a father's journey undertaken
again and again to watch over and protect
in the night, while the wind
roars outside and the stars'
blue fires burn like sapphires
around that house of memory.

2.

Grown now, both live lost and alone
in the small high rooms of tall buildings
in separate cities far away, and each night
I lumber toward those cities
but get no farther than that room
they slept in so long ago. Exhausted,
I loosen the straps of my knapsack
and set it down like another body
at their bedsides, watching them
as they were when I wished
what a father does for his daughters,
a jumble of longings I could never
put into words and knew even then
were impossible.

                So is it any wonder
that I cannot tell them by phone

what I wish for them, or at least
say something that will ease
the hurt and confusion in their words,
as sirens and horns and random shouts
enter the windows behind them
and wrestle with their voices
over the wire?

3.

        My wife,
who has similar problems with her father,
says I always imagine my daughters
as little girls asleep in that ancient room,
and only when I portray them as women
will we be able to converse in a manner
that will satisfy us all. She's right,
I'm sure, but she's not a father.

Last night I visited that room again,
but it rolled and pitched, the house
no longer a house but a ship plunging
through the night, transporting
a cargo of children all in my care
to an unknown destination. I stood
on the deck, knowing there was
no wheelhouse behind me and no rudder,
and all I could do was pray for them all,
while, like a celestial liner,
the ship slid through the night,
its hull scraped and scarred
by the hot sapphire of the stars.

SUB-DIVISION

Moonlight through the window. It is clear and cold.
As I drift into sleep, I imagine millions of insects
swarming from the dark ravine beyond the barn
towards the bulldozed orchard and the shadowy rectangles
of its half-built houses.

                        In the kitchen downstairs
the walnuts in the cut-glass bowl are dark clumps
surrounded by many sparklings and intersecting lines of light.
And in the medieval city inside each walnut,
another row of buildings leans forward and crumbles.

M & Ms

I began seeing myself
in the crowds at stadiums
and on the avenues.
I recognized who I was
because I resembled
a capital **M**:
my head lowered between
my sharply raised shoulders,
I lunged forward, refusing
to notice anyone
on either side. At times
I was a small **m**,
squat and truculent,
bulling through the crowd.
"Hey, watch it, buddy!"
It depended on my mood,
on the way I prepared
my face to meet others.
I was young: I was angry
because I didn't know
who I was or who I was
supposed to be: I was **M**
coming at you and you'd
better get out of my way.

This went on for years,
until I saw myself so often
among the multitudes—
all those **M**s grumbling
in theater audiences
or cursing among spectators
at ballgames, churches,
and political rallies—
that I realized there were others
just like me, and that **m**
was a letter which joined
with other letters
to make words, and the words

together made sentences,
and the sentences
made paragraphs, pages,
books, whole libraries;
and that in one word
or another, or by how
that word was used
in a phrase or a sentence,
I meant something else:
I was different, still **M**
but somehow always changed
by the people around me,
by the crowd shifting its weight
or altering direction.

"Excuse me," I found myself
saying. "Pardon me. Sorry,"
I said, as I elbowed my way
from one group to another.
I was overwhelmed with humility
in the presence of **M**,
which had granted me
the privilege of being
a part of all this.
It was then I swore
allegiance to **M**.
Yes, I aligned myself
with **M**, dedicated
my whole being to it.
To this day, to this moment,
I am all things **M**.
It permeates my soul.
I am **M**: it defines me
and I define it.
I can be morose or merry,
menacing or meek,
mundane or metaphysical,
masterly, moronic—or mean,
misanthropic, maudlin, manic,
monkish, mocking, mystical,
or, as I'm being now,

mischievous. Yes,
Brothers and Sisters,
I have been born again,
for **M** has shown me
I am as much a metaphor
as I am a man.

OUR STAR

Every day, whether we realize it or not,
we choose one of two stars to guide us,
a star as ephemeral as our life,
a star water can wash away. One star
is made of packed sugar, the other
of packed salt. Water melts both.
If we choose the star of sugar
we will follow all the sweet things
of the earth, the candied surfaces
that glisten, reflecting a honied light.
If salt, we will go the way of the seas—
restless, tossing broken dolls
and the timbers of drowned ships
onto everyone's shore.

                        The way of salt
is the way of sorrow and loss,
for salt seeds every tear
before it blossoms, just as death
seeds every birth. Salt is the pillar
erected to those who have looked
when they were warned not to.

At night the star illuminates our sleep,
yet before dawn it is washed away,
so that every morning we must choose again.
The poor choose the star of salt.
They break it into pieces, grind it up,
and eat it with their rough bread.
Salt is the only star in their heaven.
It is no choice at all. Invariably
the rich choose the star of sugar.
Under its light they build roads
that pass the shanties of the poor
and lead to gingerbread mansions.

I choose the star of salt. I follow it
into grocery stores and factories.
The cashiers and barbers watch me,
and the steelworkers and foreign pickers
bent over shovels or rows of lettuce.
They are silent, brooding, distrustful.
Every morning I choose their star
because it is my star also,
because it is the rich man's star,
although he doesn't know it, not yet.
Every morning I choose this star
because the salt grains hiss
on the shore as the sea washes up
the ground bones of the starless dead.

ROSES

for Wm. Grant

1.

A rose splashed
on the kitchen sink,
and then another,
a bouquet of roses
decorating
the white enamel
as if to celebrate
the blade that had
released them.

2.

I swayed,
not dizzy
from seeing
what dripped
from my finger
but from
the sight
of my body
putting forth
roses.

I pointed
that finger
like a wand
and roses
sprouted
on the counter.

Pink roses,
scarlet,
carmine,
crimson

roses, roses
edged in
odine
and ashes,
tea-colored
roses, bunches
of roses
small as
clover, roses
scattering
wherever
I pointed,
a shower
of roses
in the kitchen
as I whirled
round and round,
faster and faster,
inexplicably
dancing
in the middle
of my personal
garden
of roses.

3.

Rose of the heart
opening and closing
every second:
clock of my life
counting down to my death.

Rose of the mouth
tumbling forth words
that in praising or pondering
or tentatively defining
the edges of my life
defy my death.

Rose of the lips
that in kissing allows
my breath to entwine
with another's
and to give birth to a third
who exists
beyond my death.

Heart, mouth, lips—
roses of beginning
and end, endlessly
opening, endlessly
closing.

        4.

Roses of fire,
flame roses, roses
in the center
of fire, Roethke's
furnace roses,
"the bloody clinkers,"
rose of the fist
that must be
the center
of the universe,
fist I reach for
but cannot grasp,
fist opening
soft as a baby's
to enfold my fist
in petals of flame.

5.

If there's a God,
his tongue must be a rose
and his hands must be roses.

If there is darkness,
it must be a black rose.

If there is light
it must be the incandescence
continually igniting
in the center of the rose,
and each dawn and dusk
must be a pink or crimson
reminder of that—

                        roses
to remind us always
that this world
is a flower.

6.

And dust,
moth-winged dust,
is the dry petals
of roses pressed
in books, roses
to remember,
to commemorate,
to celebrate.

And the roses
we hold high
at the open door
when we come to visit

are a torch
to see by,
to show we care,
to say hello,
I come in peace,
I remember,
I love you.

What we express,
what we say about
the world, what we
take from the world
and give back
to it
      is roses.

2

FOREIGN PLACES

THE OLD COUNTRY

Below the steep slopes inside us
there are mountain valleys
with red-tiled roofs
surrounded by plowed fields,
staked patches of grapevine,
and domed churches
in whose tiny graveyards
the slim cypress trees
spiral toward memory.

DAWN

At sunrise
pebbles tremble,
trees shake.
Stones jostle
in an ancient hut
above a Balkan valley
where all things
that disappear
beneath the earth—
thigh bones, combs,
winecups and wedding rings—
lie hiddden, still.

Surely on such
a morning as this
the sunlight spearing
into a dark corner
must be glinting
on the lost key
that unlocks
the staircase
into the earth
where all the bones
that have disappeared
will climb once more
into the light,
singing songs
of hallelujah.

I should know better.
Each dawn
this battered planet
repairs itself
in the only way
it can—burying fists
and rusty knives.

MAJKE JEVROSIME #3

for Charles Simic

1.

The tall young Serbs are restless,
waiting in outdoor coffee bars
for the signal
to ride off against the Turks
or scramble to the mountains
where they'll harry and break
the Nazi tanks once more.
Until then, they lounge
in designer jeans,
black hair shining,
eagle eyes staring
at their iced frappes,
as they tap straws
in time to Stevie Wonder
and Madonna records
on the tape machine.

My wife and I are on the move—
we have a purpose,
albeit a peaceful one:
to find somewhere
in the heat that hangs
above the dusty boulevards
and pervades the narrow,
jig-saw puzzle streets
Majke Jevrosime #3,
Charlie Simic's birthplace.

2.

Perplexed silence channeled
through the phone wire
when I told you
I wanted to visit

this three story,
cocoa-colored building.
Once more you didn't know
if I were friend,
idolizing fan,
or lost Slavic brother
in need of encouragement
to continue on.

It's all of those, Charlie.
And make no mistake,
this *is* a pilgrimage.
It is to renew belief,
revitalize purpose
that we locate those places
where journeys meaningful
to our lives began,
or paused, or ended.
History records those events
as anonymous populations
on the move—baggage swaying,
cartwheels jolting over ruts.
But the brown eyes,
the trembling lips,
the black wen
like a punctuation mark
on the right cheek
of the thin-faced woman
cradling her four-year-old son
as the wagon rolls away
from yet another war—
that's different.
Its specific detail
destroys anonymity.
It is this house, Charlie,
or your poems.

3.

                    Only
five people are listed
in the entryway. None
are named Simic. None
know who you are
or that your family
once lived here. It is the same
with my family in Russia:
two-hundred thirty-four
men, women, and children
erased by the Nazis
and Stalin. The anonymous air
filled the vacant spaces
where they had walked and laughed,
and swept the landscape clean.
In Belgrade, Nazis,
and before them Turks,
performed similar scourings,
as though valleys and hills,
and the winds that trundled
through them, conspired
to eliminate memory—
those moments when by caressing,
punching, or imploring,
our ancestors thought
they had left an imprint,
a tiny apartment in the air
from which they would never
be evicted. That's why
our parents piled their sorrows
and complaints on us,
so we would trudge with them
into a future where their sufferings
and ours would be redeemed.

4.

Maybe that's the reason
I searched for this house,
and why, just a moment ago,
as I was about to proclaim
your presence here
in another time,
I suddenly stopped,
remembering what it is we do—
that it has been
left to us to speak
of those lost dreams
and to recall those families
who have come and gone:
Poetry is a roll call
of who those people were
and what one day
we all will be, a roll call
of names and addresses
that through our words
survive.

LUKA STANOŠ

Luka Stanoš, you took me by surprise:
how unexpected to find the year of my birth
chiseled on your tombstone in this shady graveyard
in Yugoslavia, so far away from home:

> Luka   Stanoš
> OBITELJ
> 1936-1976

On the marble headstone, your black-and-white photograph,
inside a glass bubble, stares without irony at my surprise,
head and shoulders posed at a slant like a movie star's:
wavy black hair, square face, pain-smudged eyes,
and lips, below a well-trimmed mustache, that reveal
neither a grimace nor a smile.

               Luka Stanoš, who were you?
Born the same year as I, you grew as I grew
through summers and winters of Hitler and Mussolini,
although your childhood was not spent
knowing that cloudbanks out at sea
hid a distant war. Your war was as close
as the foreign men who slept in your bed,
forcing you to sleep on the floor—
their growling language at the table,
their black boots and gray wool uniforms,
their glinting rifle breeches smooth with sour oil.
For five years the grapes swelled, the valley bloomed,
then withered, then bloomed again,
and in every season the wind licked a long tongue
under your bedroom door. While you and your friends
played tag and the German soldiers watched,
helmets off, smiling and cheering your every move,
I listened to the radio underneath my pillow
and knew Jack Armstrong and General Eisenhower
would win the war. Did you pray the Partisans
would come and kill the Nazi *svinja*?
Did you cheer for them?

                    Truman, Stalin, Tito;
sixth grade, seventh: I could barely read,
didn't know my times table past the 6s.
Did you excel in history and grammar?
Did you listen to Roy Orbison sing
about his pretty woman in the '60s
and smile at a woman of your own?
Did the Beatles make you imagine all the people
you would never know? And did you suspect, even once,
that through all those years each of us, on opposite sides
of the planet, was growing separately yet the same
toward our different deaths?

                    How did you die?
An auto accident? A fall, head first, against a stone?
The old woman who we've come to visit,
my wife's great aunt, says you had been ill for years—
cancer, she thought—and that your death
was a blessing in the end to both family and friends.
Luka Stanoš, you were trudging inevitably to 1976,
to forty years packed in the crate of your body
that in the end was packed in the earth,
leaving this marble gravestone and your photograph.

I turn to walk away and then turn back,
conscious of each step that will take me from you,
aware that once again our lives must separate
and I shamble toward a date I do not know,
already thirteen years beyond your caring.

Luka, give me a sign: make a branch fall,
a pebble drop, a swallow screech and wing away—
something to let me know where all of us are headed,
something to tell me that all this suffering,
all this uncertainty, are for a reason.
No, of course not. Silence, even in the trees.
What answers I receive will come from the living,
not the dead; I know that. Nor does this meeting

obligate me to do those things you never did
for the rest of every hour, month, and year
that I continue to breathe the planet's souring air.

It's time to go. This has been a stopping place
on a sunny afternoon where for a moment things are clear—
a place worth marking on any map. Luka Stanoš,
I take my leave, but do not leave you here.

LOOKING FOR VASKO POPA

Nothing could be less appropriate
than to think of Eliot's winding stair
as I grope my way from landing to landing
in this old apartment house in Belgrade.
The stairs are unlit, and for three floors
I follow a shadowy elevator's iron cage,
shuffling through tumble-down plaster,
newspapers, bottles, and cellophane,
sniffing collapsed oranges and sour wine,
cigarette smoke, oiled machinery, and grime
before I arrive at the old poet's door.

He isn't home. I knock again and listen,
imagining him in a room down a dusty hall,
helpless in a chair, his eyes bulging
as he struggles to work his lips.
Listen, there is only the drone of wind
beneath the door, and again I think of Eliot,
his final silence echoing down his last years
as down a stairwell like this one,
where he saw himself as an old man
still gripping the banister at the bottom step.

Downstairs a plump little shopkeeper,
who speaks no English, grips his thigh
and hops to the right, trying to tell me,
with whistles and grunts, that the poet
broke his leg and has been convalescing
hundreds of miles away, at the seaside.
Images of Eliot rise again: the Fisher King
revitalized, with slashes on his thigh—
imprinted impotence in a hop,
a stutter step, that is one of the meanings
the shopkeeper's pantomime ludicrously implies.
The other is the absence here of a poet's
precise use of words to perfectly describe
the all too apparent imperfection of men.

To think of Eliot at a time like this:
nothing could be less fitting than the dry,
deliberate poetics of the English don
in comparison to the poet I search for here,
a maker of ten-page epics, where bones
don't chirp but comically debate, pliers
with broken jaws, like discarded workmen,
are thrown out of windows, and the combined
sides of triangles, sliding on fiery tracks,
equal human destiny.

                        And yet, and yet—
both poets walked among the multitudes
and looked for meaning after major wars,
the Englishman in old books and rusty symbols,
arriving in the end at the arthritic ceremonies
of a doddering church, while this poet,
whose apartment is approached by stumbling
through the rubbish of an age, found meaning
in his native folklore and the fellowship
of mountain fighters defending their land.
All this he compressed into a pristine music,
chimes of sunlight and wind pinging
over an endless line of refugees—
a raised arm, a hammer flying into the air,
an eye peeking from behind a cart.
He made a mythology of this, his people's history:
populations fleeing for their lives,
slaughtering others or those in their ranks,
or flowing through the landscape
on an endless pilgrimage—human parts
seen for a moment and then gone,
as in a crowd we glimpse a shoulder
or the swagger of someone familiar,
or watch a teapot roll from a thicket of legs,
which hands immediately grab, returning it
to the anonymous mass of moving bodies.

He distilled these elements into cosmic yawns
and magic kettles, added the star charts
glinting in the joints of every skeleton,
and made of them all a secondary heaven.
He never abandoned these images of the lost,
now pliers crushing a nail's head,
now pebbles and triangles scurrying
after their gluttonous, comic-book ends,
until he seemed to live in a huge room,
surrounded by clocks and discarded flywheels,
where broken lips and overturned eyeballs—
once the smiles and frightened eyes of dolls—
littered the floor around his easy chair,
and runaway teeth, galloping in cavalry charges
back and forth across the carpet, dashed
headlong into the walls, scattering like dice
before they re-formed their clattering ranks
in readiness for yet another charge.
All the while, the poet did not dare to move,
afraid he might trample his tiny charges or knock over
the miniature kettles and dancing shoes
on the table near his elbow. Nor could he
call out in a voice that might deafen them,
even to answer the pounding down the hall
where someone was knocking on his apartment door.

ST. MARK'S CATHEDRAL, BELGRADE (1989)

- 1 -

        Dome upon dome,
        and God—where is He?
        As in a shell game,
        the pea, hidden
        beneath this one,
        that one, or maybe
        that other one,
        reveals Him to be
        nowhere you thought.

The Byzantines hoisted one dome
on another, making the game
more complex, a succession of domes
swimming in air, each one
harboring winds or maybe
the whisper of the Eternal Voice,
a moan more (or less) earthly
than the soul in torment.

The priests learned to use
these inverted cups by sending
choired hymns of hallelujah
into the highest dome, the sound
spiraling and trapped, vibrant
beneath that hard sky, like birds
in midflight stopped miles
from their destination, hovering,
still for a moment, then vanishing.

And they painted the walls and domes
with bright colors—scenes of Christ
ascendant, entering Jerusalem,
or breaking the marble doors of Death
with his naked foot, his body swathed
in cloth the color of apricots.

The robes of saints were fiery sheets
of blood, a glossy vermillion hard
as lacquerware, their gowns lemon,
celery green, or prune brown, the sheen
of their cloaks a metallic blue.

In a ravine, Elijah, seated on a rock,
head in hand, elbow on knee,
wearing a luminescent milk-blue gown
under a scarlet cloak trimmed
in brown fur, contemplates the raven
who fed him at God's command.

Mary, wearing an eggplant-purple robe,
is informed by Gabriel—winged, wrapped
in gray, the creases of his garment
shooting rays of silver—that she
has been chosen as Christ's mother.

And blue everywhere: sapphire blue,
lavender-, peacock-, hyacinth blue,
air blue, heaven-and-sea blue.
And all the while, the Voice of God
everywhere and nowhere, grunts
or indecipherable mutterings
that reverberate high inside the dome.

- 2 -

In Belgrade, St. Mark's cathedral,
surrounded by trees and park,
resembles a group of shoulders
bowed in prayer. It is immense,
its many domes still making it
the most striking building
on the dusty, tree-lined avenue
now called Revolution Boulevard.

Inside, the central dome, rising
two hundred feet above the floor,
is aimed, it seems, at heaven.
But the walls are gray, dank
as a dungeon, every saint
and divine act hacked, scraped,
or peeled from the surface,
the plaster chipped and splotched
with stains that darken the walls,
the whole interior reminiscent
of those places prisoners are led
and, as they watch, are one
at a time, or in groups of three,
with pistols or by firing squads, shot.

Still the people come, lining up
to purchase candles at the kiosk
just inside the door before they creep
in the dim light to niche or altar
where some patron saint—his power
pulsing from a faded plaque
or shriveled bone—bestows his presence,
if not his blessing, on their prayers,
something they can carry back
to their cramped, state-owned apartments
to wish on, much as their grandparents
in their huts had done. To all of them
the church is still efflorescent inside,
and the droning hymns and humble saints
are still garbed in red and green and pray
on walls of translucent light,
so that all who enter here still imagine
they are enclosed in the chamber
of a miraculous, bee-blessed flower
glowing among all the other flowers
in the middle of Paradise.

                Dome upon dome,

and God—where is He?
As in a shell game,
the pea, hidden
beneath this one,
that one, or maybe
that other one,
reveals Him to be
nowhere you thought.

LETTER TO CZESLAW MILOSZ

Dear Czeslaw,

                I just discovered we were neighbors long ago.
It was in Vilna, where you had gone to school
those early years before I was born.
It was in Vilna, where I have never been.
You who have navigated so often between here and there,
then and now, understand me, I'm sure.
My great-grandfather on my mother's side,
a merry little man, was a dealer in oil and grain.
His brother owned a mill just north of town, on the river.
Either could have been the old Galician Jew
who told you that anyone who was right all the time
was neither brilliant nor holy but merely fanatical.
The grain dealer, his brother, and their children,
in fact that whole side of the family,
went up in smoke at about the same time as Lithuania
and the ghetto in Warsaw.

                My grandfather
was a laborer, cap and dusty workman's apron.
Had you passed him on the street, you would not have noticed him
as he hauled iron or loaded wagons in the cobbled gutter.
Besides, he was gone before you arrived with your school-boy's face
to prepare for a life for which there was no preparation.
He had gone to an America you have never seen—
tenements with sour body gases and the stink
of stewed cabbage wafting through the halls, the daily clink
of coins inside a jar. For him, America was not much different
from Vilna, except, he said, that here he could stretch at times,
give his body ease in a way that was inconceivable at "home."
Of course, his children flourished in this America,
inhabiting the landscape and the air
as if it were their own, which, I know,
is a mistake my people have made before.
The old man never made it to California.
That was left for me to do, and you as well.
And so we are neighbors once again, here

at the end of the American continent:
one from the pages of Augustine and Pascal,
the other from the Baal Shem and shopmen's ledgers.

I, too, have read Cabeza de Vaca, and followed him,
dragged and kicked by worshipping redskins,
across the uncharted territories
currently identified as Louisiana and Texas.
And I, too, wondered at his return to a Europe
of tapestries and side chapels, rubies and gold;
of silken insteps arching above a candlelit floor.
And like you, I preferred the war whoop
and ripping wild radishes from the unexplored land.

Still, I continually look over my shoulder
as if to make sure that where I have come from
is still there, although I know it isn't.
Know?—a strong if blunt and undistinguished word
with the face of a peasant or a potato,
or one of those "redskin brothers" whom Father Junipero
found with "reason and memory dimmed. . . ."

I'm sure you've noticed in supermarkets
packages of meat and containers of milk
marked *perishable,* as if to warn the buyer
not to dwell on the present beyond its day.
What's past is past, the labels admonish us—
it's best to remember that neither chops
nor short ribs can stay. Still, those streets
in Vilna—were they really cobbled? Did hooves
strike sparks like silver bells against them,
which woke the guardian mole below like thunder?
Was—is—that old Galician Jew and all his years
of accumulated wisdom buried beneath those streets,
and is he—hunched in his cavern,
endlessly reading from the great book of human history—
the one to whom the victims, as well as the executioners,
are, sooner or later, answerable. . .?

THE BOY IN THE PAINTING

The boy in the painting is blowing
on a broken branch, holding the fiery end
like a candle: level with his lips, close to his chin.
There is darkness all around, but the glowing ember
lights his face and arms, although the darkness
surrounds him like the silence in a bell jar.
It is a silence so deep, I can almost hear
the passage of his exhaled breath—and it engenders
a moment so poised, it has become a pause
that makes me stop before the painting
with a start.

            Knowing the painter's dates
and place of residence, I think the scene
is Lunéville, 1645, in the duchy of Lorraine,
which for ten years has been burned and pillaged
in the Thirty Years War, and where plague
as well as soldiers in harness with clanking swords,
their metal breastplates glinting in the firelight,
have hacked and hammered the populace,
leaving rubble and the cries of women in their wake.

Such knowledge makes the silence in the painting
echo through the darkened theater in my head,
where without his leather jerkin and velvet sleeves
the boy could be one of the same four actors
I always envision, who follow one another
onto the dimly lighted stage: first a youth deep in a cave
who stares in wonder at the the deer and bison
painted like a zodiac on the enclosing walls.
Next a political prisoner waking startled in his cell,
suddenly aware that the graffiti scrawled
by countless others are the only stars around his bed.
Then an old man come to his final rest
whose last shout is his whole life, a torch—
thrown against the darkness—that for an instant
slides like a falling star across the night.
Last is the woman in the marketplace
who pokes among the cabbages and grapes,
unware that her womb is the cave, cell, universal night
from which we fall, all of us, into the blinding light.

THE CHINESE IMMIGRANT'S LAMENT

If I am old now
I feel no different
than when I was young
and new in this place
and thought I was a chunk
of my homeland
broken off and exported
for a foreigner's
profit or pleasure—
the body of a teapot
with a soul of silk.

It was more, much more
than being a stranger here.
It was as if I had been ripped
from the earth in a flood,
carried by restless seas,
and thrown on the shores
of this distant land
like some gasping creature
you stared at
more in bewilderment
than disbelief.

Your stares nudged me
like a boot determining
if I was real, or you laughed
at my looks and clothes
and different ways,
thinking they gave you
the right to order me about
for your most menial tasks,
and to teach me how
to pray and think and do
everything just like you.

Now I want to be buried
in my homeland,
interred with the dust
of my ancestors, a dust
I'll wear like a silk robe,
for the pain of separation
I've carried clenched
inside me all these years
will unroll like a bolt
of the finest cloth and I'll
wrap myself in it like a cocoon.

You with your foreign eyes,
what do you know
about the world that goes on
behind this face
so impassively turned
toward you? My heart
breaks into pieces
as easily as that dish
you so casually place
on your dining room table
and call china.

AFTER THE END

1. Penelope

Every night at my weaving in the room above,
I imagined the men I heard below
drunk in the great hall—their sweaty chests
and hairy hands, their belching laughter,
buckles and swords. I steered this into my weaving
as into a net of nerves and memory—not meaning to,
but forgetting the design, if I ever knew it;
knowing only my intentions—that in the morning
I would unravel all I had composed
the night before. For twenty years I wove
every pattern my mind could conjure,
fragments of past, present, and possible futures.
But his return was like nothing I had imagined:
the bodies pitched over the upturned tables,
the warm blood thigh deep and he greasy with it
and grizzled in the doorway, grinning
past me to the bed. At first I thought
he was one of them, a foreigner fierce
from all that waiting and ready to force
his frustrations on the frayed web
of my threadbare feelings and, surprisingly,
I shivered with expectation and delight.

Months later, years, when I was wife again,
I could not forget the nights of weaving
when the oil lamps' flames flared wild
as wings against the walls and my fingers,
fluttering at the loom as if it were a lyre,
wove impossible possibilities.
His return had stopped all that, yanked the yarn
to scattered strings, as though with the death
of each man in the great hall below
had died a conceivable direction.
Now I know what I did not know then—
the regret that keeps me for hours each night
lying sleepless at his snoring side.

2. Odysseus

For twenty years I was gone on that journey,
guided only by guile and star charts and the gods
whose grudges left me weeping for home—this rocky island
as anonymous as sleep without dreams,
where day after day the same waves
crawl and mutter against the stones, like servants
who beg to be forgiven in a foreign tongue.
And, yes, I killed them all when I returned,
all the suitors in the great hall, and even then
I trembled with excitement as the long bow quivered
like a lyre in my hands, making an unexpected music
among all that shouting and blood
and the fallen who groaned.

                         Each day
I sit on this promontory, looking out to sea,
expecting a ship to arrive or a beast
to burst from the water. But the sea remains
flat and uninspired. I cannot conjure
anything but memory from the waves,
a more and more tepid twitch in my tranquil blood.
But once—once? Did it really happen,
or was it a dream unraveling in my head
like the weavings she says she undid each day I was gone?

She's up there now, in the drafty halls,
still waiting for whatever it is she expects me to say:
"Lady, I missed you. . . Lady, it was thoughts of you. . ."
And that is true, all true. But the gods and their grudges
had saved the worst of the tortures for last: this place
which I longed for and she whose presence
I could not live without, both turned now
into a tedium I trip on, like scattered yarn
that clutches at my ankles and hobbles my steps,
tying me to a tapestry from which I cannot escape.

"ONCE I WOKE"

Once I woke with a woman in a gorge on the island of Crete
at the moment the moon edged over the cliff above us.
All around, weeds released their spicy scents
as if the earth was exhaling all its worries.

We both sat up at the same instant, as if pushed
from our dreams, as if we were meant to stream
with plant-breath and insect wings all the way to heaven.
Bits of things rose around us, a heavy dust
seething and hissing.

                    Afterwards, we sat in our bodies
gazing at one another. And in the silence,
in the clear moonlight, we stared at the stones, the weeds,
and everything else that had been left behind.

YEAR AFTER YEAR

- 1 -

Stars as large as snowflakes
hang above the town. The dogs
look up and whimper,
and the roads disappear
and reappear among the dark hills.

In town, a sudden chill
enters the open windows,
along with the scent of barley
harvested the week before.
The women, crocheting, look up,
and so do the men, cards raised
above their heads, cards ready to be
snapped down on the wooden tables.
Someone is playing a piano
in a house several blocks away—
a woman—and everyone hears her voice
singing the piano's plaintive song.

Blind and expressionless,
the old sit in corners and listen,
while thieves shove knives in their sashes
and when no one is looking
slip from the houses,
shushing the dogs outside.

They will wait by the side
of the chalky roads, faces lost
in shadow or every so often peeping
from the trees like white lanterns,
as they stare at a cemetery on the hill
opposite their hiding place,
where pine trees are black flames
swaying above luminous tombstones.

- 2 -

Year after year I wake unnerved
from this scene. And always
I turn from the lighted rooms
to the thieves hiding at roadside,
and try to hear and see what they do—
the breeze, the faint sound
of a woman singing, the cemetery,
encrusted with moonlight,
silent on the hill opposite.

                          It is not so much
what the thieves are doing here
that engages my attention,
as the way they perceive the night,
so different from those in town:
they wait for the sounds of horsemen
or rattling coaches—sounds
that will bring the townspeople
to stand at their open windows,
looking toward the darkened roads.

If these are the moments I return to,
it is always with the awareness
of those innumerable blue-white hours,
just before dawn, when the townspeople
are dreaming in their beds
and the thieves, unshaven and hollow-eyed,
sneak back to town, signalling
the dogs to remain quiet
as they enter their houses
on aching feet, the unused knives
still stuck through their sashes.

- 3 -

It is never clear why the stars
are so large over this town,
why the dogs are upset, or why
the barley-scented chill
ripples through the windows.
It is never clear what the woman
is singing, or whether the same woman
sings every night, any more than
whether the thieves are the same
or whether the men playing cards,
or the crocheting women, or the old,
the infirm, the blind, take their place
by the side of the road, knives
glinting in their cummerbunds—
even whether the town is at peace
or in the midst of a revolution,
whether the thieves station themselves
in the shadows nightly or wait
for a specific shipment to pass their way,
a shipment of gold or arms that will
set them free; or whether they wait
for news from a distant city
of seige, or plague, or earthquake.

- 4 -

All that is clear are the moments
we wait in the dark by the side
of the road, sniffing barley,
quivering from a sudden chill,
and hearing in the distance
a woman's melancholy song,
while the stars—so large,
like snowflakes—shine
above the luminous cemetery
on the hill across the way.

3
THE GLORIOUS DEAD

RABELAIS, 1553

Rabelais in a coma for three days.
When the death rattle enters his throat,
his eyes spring open, his snarled beard shakes,
and lifting himself from the pillows
he sweeps from his chest the six-foot cross,
all brass and heavy as a bedstead,
which the presumptuous priests,
now chanting around him, had placed there,
and before falling back in the bedclothes,
he exclaims, "Curtain! The farce is ended!
And now off to a vast perhaps."

HAYDN, 1772

Haydn conducting the first performance
of the "Farewell Symphony" for Count Esterhazy
in his palace, the work composed so that
here and there an instrument would cease,
each bewigged and bespectacled musician
pack up his case and depart, the rich sounds
in that great hall, with its plaster curlicues
and cherubs and six-foot candelabras, diminishing
like candles going out one by one in a chandelier,
until the last musician, the composer himself,
closed the door behind him. That moment
when the door closes, leaving the count,
second only to the Emperor in property and power,
seated on his red-plush, gilt-edged throne,
his hushed courtiers looking toward him,
his lands tilled and tidy beyond the palace:
—that moment when the count leans forward
and stares at the music stands and empty chairs.

SHELLEY'S FUNERAL

On the beach near Viareggio,
Trelawny burned Shelley's corpse
on a funeral pyre he had designed
made of black iron—an open grate
above an enclosed firebox,
like a hoodless baby buggy with handles
instead of wheels. Byron and Hunt
remained in their carriage, watching.
A health officer from Leghorn
and four dragoons were also present
that sultry day in August, 1822.
It took hours for the corpse to burn,
even though the pyre was peach-pink
and the flames roared inside. Finally,
in the saffron dusk, when "the largest bones
had been reduced to white cinders,"
the body was formless, nothing but ashes.
However, Shelley's heart would not burn,
"although bedded in fire," Trelwany wrote.
"There was a bright flame around it. . .
and after sprinkling it with sea water
I took the heart in my hand
to examine it, but it was still so hot
as to burn my hand badly."

Later Byron wrote to his friend Moore:
"All of Shelley was consumed, except the heart. . . ."

BALZAC, 1850

Paris. August 18, 1850.
His face black, his body
a swollen sack of gangrene,
Honoré de Balzac, in the end,
muttered, "Send for Bianchon."
Evelina Hanska, who for years
refused to marry him
until he pursued her
that spring into the Ukraine,
had gone to bed. His mother
sat beside him, watching
this sputtering torch
of suet and muscle,
her fifty-one-year-old son,
until recently a great devourer
of food and women and the creator
of a nation in his novels,
and heard him say,
"Send for Bianchon,"
and sat there, unable to respond,
knowing that Bianchon
was, it's true, a doctor,
but a doctor in her son's
monumental novels,
La Comedie Humaine.

QUARTET IN A MINOR KEY

1. Schumann

They knew Robert Schumann was mad
and had to be locked in an asylum
when every sound he heard
was "transformed into music. . .
with instruments of splendid resonance
never heard on earth before. . . ."
That was on February 15th, 1854.
On the night of the seventeenth
the composer wandered about Dusseldorf,
eyes raised as he listened
to the angelic music struck
from wagon wheels and horseshoes,
from boot soles slapping cobblestones,
from passersby clearing their throats,
bickering, kissing, sighing.

By the twenty-first, the music had turned
into a coven of shrieking witches
and he was afraid he would hurt
his children and his beloved Clara.
On the twenty-seventh, he ran without shoes
into the rain and leaped
from a bridge into the Rhine.
The townspeople fished him out
and led him home, his hands
hiding his face, as they muttered
wasn't he ashamed, and with
such a fine family too,
come, come, Herr Schumann,
you must get hold of yourself.

Two years later, he died in his sleep
at a private asylum in Endenich,
after days of striding around his room
in arm-waving arguments
with unseen spirits.
In the end, Clara—whom he

hardly recognized but who remembered
that once "he put his arm around me:
and not for all earthly treasure
would I exchange that embrace"—
his precious Clara, had to observe him
through a closed window.

2. Clara

After Robert Schumann went mad and died
in the asylum, Clara, then thirty-seven
and a renowned pianist,
toured Europe playing his music
for the remainder of her life:
She never remarried.

                I always see her
in her later years, a small German woman
seated before the crouching black beast
of her husband's madness:

                      Every night
for forty years the beast would feed
from the frail but determined Clara's hands,
squatting before her as she tickled
and stroked it, teased and coaxed it
to murmur and chortle, growl and roar
those sounds that made her beloved Robert,
whom the beast had swallowed whole,
live again, as she tapped at its teeth
and eased from under its glossy shell
the sounds of the lover she remembered,
who could be touched only in this way,
although she never understood
that neither beast nor lover
could exist without the other.

3. Brahms

Brahms caught a chill from which he never recovered
at Clara Schumann's funeral outside Frankfurt

on a gray day in 1896. He had loved her
even when Robert was still alive, had loved her
for more than forty years, ever since he was twenty,
a love that Clara, still enamored with her long-dead Robert,
reciprocated with friendship and professional encouragement.

That day Brahms the bachelor, the corpulent composer,
turned toward his own death from Clara's grave
because hope was now behind him, because his music—
suddenly a sack of fighting cats—was also behind him.

The doctor said, "Cancer of the liver," but from that gray day
at the cemetery, the chill that shook him
as he stood a Clara's grave side, the shiver
that passed like a hand over his entire body,
never seemed to depart. Within the year,
he took to his bed. On April 2nd, 1897,
he lay unconscious all day with his face to the wall.
On April 3rd, he turned over with a shudder and died.

4. The Housekeeper

The woman who nursed Brahms in his last years
is usually referred to as his *housekeeper*.
After all, she wrote no music and played
no instruments: of what importance was her name?

For twenty-five years she looked after the composer:
washed his socks, prepared his meals,
and emptied the cigar stubs from his ashtrays,
while he thought only of Clara.

                            This housekeeper
remained with Brahms to the end, feeding him soups
and changing his bedclothes. The only talent
she seemed to possess was unconditional devotion.
We know her name was Celestine Truxa,
but no one saw fit to record the manner of her death.

A LETTER (1885)

for Wm. Grant

December 21, 1885
Markt-St. Florian,
Austria

Dear Sophie,
               Bruckner, that great good man,
plumper than in the photographs, and shorter,
but with that famous nose fixed in his face
like the hooked beak of some prehistoric turtle,
returned through the early morning from a stroll
and entered the doorway of the farmhouse kitchen.
He brought the cold clear morning with him.
It swirled into the room like attending angels
smelling of milk and wood smoke. Bits of straw
stuck to his jacket, a rough black homespun.
His ears glowed from the sunlight behind him,
and snowy peaks were just visible in the distance
over his shoulders, as he steamed and stamped,
not saying a word when he found us here,
where we had been waiting unannounced.
He was so much an emissary of the landscape,
which hovered like a crystal cathedral at his back,
that we were breathless at his entrance
and could only mutter, "Maestro, Maestro,"
awkward and confused as schoolboys—
a captain of the guard, named Brunner; Richter, the conductor;
and my lowly self, who as district manager
was representing the firm, since Herr Gutmann
had taken ill the previous day. The Captain
handed Bruckner the scroll we had been sent to deliver.
Bruckner read it and frowned, still standing all ashimmer
from the outdoors, as if that instant he had stepped
from another world, and for a moment
I thought we had presented the document
to the wrong person, that this was not the house;
that all the hurried preparation in offices and streets,
all that clatter of horse-drawn carriages

and wooden wagon wheels jolting over clamorous cobbles,
that stiff snap of frozen leather and hammering hooves,
slapping harnesses and jouncing chains
over the ice-packed country roads—had brought us
to the wrong place. And what, after all,
could we have given this shy, good man
that would have been of any value to him,
that would have made him do anything but frown
as he did then, turning the parchment over,
as if the other side would somehow explain
what it all meant and who we were
seated in his kitchen so early in the day.
We must have looked a sight, our faces haggard from the trip
that at the Emperor's bidding we had made without delay,
all night through fog and sleet and gusty winds,
and whose purpose we had quite forgotten
seeing Bruckner stout and steaming in the doorway,
even at that moment surrounded by a slight mist,
as if he had brushed against a column of heavenly masonry
just before re-entering the confines of our world.
What, really, could be said at such a moment,
except by the Captain, who stepped forward,
clicked his heels, and exclaimed, "The Emperor Franz Joseph
extends his greetings and invites you. . ." and stopped,
for Bruckner had smiled, shrugged, and opened his hands
as if he couldn't comprehend the language, or was deaf,
and stood there meekly like a prisoner
who agreed to come along without a fuss
although he didn't understand the charges.
All this happened just as an icy wind sailed
through the doorway from the gothic mountains,
blowing the feathers of invisible angels into our faces.

I will tell you more of this when I return
from locating that wayward shipment of Chopin etudes
and Czerny lesson books in Salzburg, and settling
my semi-annual accounts in Steyr and Linz.

Until then, I remain,
                    Your respectful fiance,
                                        Wilhelm

CHEKHOV'S FUNERAL

Moscow, July, 1904. On that hot and dusty day,
tens of thousands thronged the boulevards
or waited at the station for Chekhov's coffin,
then followed the procession—led by an honor guard
of mounted cavalry—to the Virgin's Cemetery,
only to find they had accompanied the remains
of a General Keller coming from Manchuria.
Chekhov's coffin arrived in a green freight car
marked FOR OYSTERS in giant letters on the side.
Fewer than a hundred people followed the hearse,
dawdling behind a fat policeman who led the way
seated imperiously on a white horse.
Two lawyers, in spats and speckled ties,
bickered about the brain power of dogs.
Someone else extolled the comforts of his country home.
And ladies, twirling fringed umbrellas
on their shoulders, whispered about Countess M.
and Mrs. D., and eyed the well-attired men.
Surely, this was a story Chekhov would have written
with his grave simplicity, tenderness, and sad smile.

RODIN & RILKE: MEUDON, 1902

Rodin
was a hands on
kind of guy.
When Rilke
became his secretary
there was no way
the poet could tip-toe
behind a door
or take himself
into a land
of crystal
chandeliers.

"Feel that,"
the bull-nosed
sculptor would say,
smacking
the marble ass
of a half-formed
nymph, and Rilke,
with a hand
as soft as
a lily, would reach
out a trembling
finger like Adam
in the painting.

It was as much
a reaching in
as a reaching out.
That's what the sculptor,
a father forty years
the poet's senior,
and all thumbs,
failed to see.

In the end,
they couldn't stand
each other,
but that was
several years
of half-formed asses
down the road.

THE BLESSING

Every evening at six, Gorky entered his office,
tall and lanky, almost stoop-shouldered,
with his high cheekbones and walrus mustache,
and his blue eyes burning like sapphires.
Naval officers waited for him, factory workers,
peasants and princesses, all clutching
their manuscripts. He whispered to each one,
took their notebooks or handed notebooks back.
This was in St. Petersburg in 1915,
at the editorial offices of *Letopis* magazine.
Babel was one who came, unpublished, starving,
without an overcoat, a chubby twenty-year-old
in a city winter where it was ten below.
Gorky had taken his stories three days before.
They were dog-earred, tea-stained, and smudged.
After the others had gone, Gorky invited the boy
into his office and settled behind the desk.
"There are little nails and big nails," he said.
"A writer must walk barefoot over them,
mostly over the big ones. A writer's whole life
is spent walking barefoot over nails.
But if he is honest, both as man and writer,
he will consider it an honor to trudge that path.
I waited until the others had left to wish you luck
on this journey, and to give you my blessing."

CELINE, 1951

Cold sunlight through high windows
on a February day in nineteen-fifty-one:
Celine, standing in a Paris courtroom,
guilty of treason, turns from the judge
to all those vengeful faces in the crowd,
his lean, pock-marked features unrepentant,
and quietly, but with metallic clarity, says,
"I piss on you all from a great height."

A TRIPTYCH FOR GIACOMETTI

1. The Epiphany

One evening in the 1920s
when Giacometti was at a movie show,
the figures on the screen disintegrated
to black and white specks shifting
on a surface without depth.
Outside, everything "appeared different:
wondrous, transformed, entirely new."
Until then, his vision of the world
"as it was for everyone" was photographic.
Now "I began to see heads in a void,
in a space which surrounds them.
I clearly perceived how a head
I was looking at could become fixed,
immobilized definitively in time.
It was no longer a living head
but an object like no other, something
simultaneously living and dead.
I gave a cry of terror, as if entering
a world no one had seen before.
All the living were dead in the subway,
in the street, in the restaurant where I ate.
The waiter at the Brasserie Lipp
became immobile leaning toward me,
with his mouth open and eyes fixed
between the moment that had just passed
and the moment that came after it."

2. "City Square" (1948)

His emaciated stick figures
are vanishing into the Void,
never meeting, never saying "hello,"
always about to become
nothing, to step into nowhere
out of a past that is stripped

away from them like clothing,
like their expressions and names
when the flesh is gone
and only the skeleton remains.

We stroll across a city square.
Five others stroll nearby, each walking
at a forty-five degree angle to the others—
so we can never meet, or even see
one another's eyes. This is how
we crisscross the square,
walking endlessly toward someone
we endlessly miss, each of us
reduced to a diagonal route,
like a horse unable to prance
in a straight line, or a chess piece
whose movement cannot be changed
without destroying the game.

3. The End

Giacometti's mother died at ninety-three.
That day, the sixty-four-year-old sculptor
sat in his studio all afternoon and crooned
through the night, rocking back and forth
in the space alloted him, totally alone,
at first mumbling to himself, then calling
in his mother's voice, as raspy as a crow's,
"Alberto, come eat. Alberto, come eat."

SUFFERING

I don't know if it's human to suffer,
or if we suffer because we're human,
or because God hates a part of himself
or because we hate a part of ourselves
we call "God" or "cancer" or "misery".
Forget the devil, or evil. They're too easy.
We learn from our uncles with arthritis,
Aunt Nora with the cancer she grips
to the center of her chest like a locket,
staring out the bedroom window
as if looking for the lost lover
I knew was not a lover but her life.
Did she see it lumbering down the block,
carrying away the sack of her memories—
the son splattered in the ball turret
of the B-17, the daughter, pregnant,
twisting on the rusty coat hanger
in the apartment on Church Street
that belonged to the bald little doctor
with hairy forearms and rolled up sleeves?

The children in Zambia and India,
their arms and legs like broken twigs
around their empty, swollen bellies;
the grandfather set on fire by his neighbors;
the daughter whose face is stapled with shrapnel;
the cancer patient watching the IV
as if it were a clock ticking away her life—
I don't need to write you a list, I'm sure.
You've got your own list, ranked top
to bottom with your own examples,
or maybe not ranked, maybe not even
under the same heading: My "Sufferings"
could be your "Failures," "Desires,"
"Goals," "Future Plans," "Things To Do,"
as if the heart attack or car crash
never planned for, will never happen.
As if your husband will not leave you,

or your wife run off with your best friend
or your lover go, or, in the end, your children,
grandchildren, fortune, memory, breath.

The Buddhists say the need for anything
is suffering: whatever we desire, or just want,
will cling to us like an oppressive shadow
that we'll never be able to shake off,
even when we feel its head in our mouth,
feeding on our breath. It's our expectations:
those lists of goals and things to do
that do us in. And I'm not just talking
about love, sex, money, or rich stews
simmering in brown gravy. There were
the things we never thought to mention
that we didn't want. It wasn't on my list
to grow old and grouchy and full of pain,
nor could I foresee AIDS and now Ebola
inflating men, women and children
and bursting them everywhere like bubbles
full of sewage. Even the Buddhists
never figured out that in needing nothing
they were needing not to need,
which, on the face of it, is pretty needy.

Jesus said, "Suffer the little children
to come unto me." That was scary enough.
But then God, his father, made him suffer for us all.
And remember his last words on the Cross?
I mean, if you can't trust Him, who can you trust?
"The only thing we can be sure of in this life,"
the smirkiest of my high school buddies
said, "is that in the end we're going to die,"
to which the sergeant in boot camp added,
"You'll never see the bullet with your name on it.
But since you begin to die the moment
you're born anyway, why worry?"
All these thoughts: how are we supposed
to plan our days, not to mention the next hour?
Then I think of that interview on television:
When asked how she coped with the deaths

of both her children within a two-year period,
the actress said, "We breathe instinctively,"
and sat there, at peace. Every so often
we need to remember something this simple.

4

SHOUTING DOWN THE SILENCE

TONGUE

Tongue, wild meat rose
surrounded by carrion breath,
our one wing struggling to take flight,
wing in the head the body grips
and won't let fly: Tongue
that hisses, Tongue that sings,
Tongue that flops, that flaps,
that stabs inside its cage,
that articulates gasps and cries
and those long passages of breath
that would escape without hope
or chance of salvation:

                              Tongue, Tongue,
if there's one thing in the body
that defines us, it's you.
You are the wild flame
that leaps at the stars
from a campfire at night,
as though the face that owned you
were the Earth's chapped skin.
You leap so high, so bright,
what does it matter if in the end
you must fall among charred stones
like a sucked-in breath?

When God said, "Let there be light, "
his tongue leaped through the dark
to make clear what he had said.
That is why old women marvel
at each new word a child exclaims:
the mouth cracks open as if the head
were an egg, and tentative
yet impudent the tiny pink wing tip
thrusts into the light.

THE CELL

Through a microscope
I saw a cell
in a drop of water
spread radiant-edged
in one direction
rather than several others:
sliding, creeping—
a robe, it seemed,
with a soul inside.
Then it twitched,
the cell twitched,
a movement
no more than a wink
yet, in reality,
a kick more violent
than a galaxy shuddering—
and suddenly bigbacked
the cell wrenched in two:
a seam made visible,
an agony of edges
crawling away
from each other
like continents
heaving apart,
and Brother, I murmured
to each new cell, Brother.

To this I bear witness:
I was twelve.
The wonder filled
both my eyes,
although only one eye
saw it, because now
both eyes were brothers,
because now both hands
were friends
who worked together
in the fields, and my feet

an inseparable pair
likely to dance off
in any direction.

At twenty I was shown
how the brain
flies apart like two hands
thrown wide in rapture
under the impact
of a government issue
.45. The man
who demonstrated this
looked nothing like me,
although we were dressed
in the same uniform and spoke
the same language,
and Brother, I murmured
to him, Brother.
And Brother, I murmured
to the boy whose head
had just come apart
and in whose face
I recognized my own.

It is to this dichotomy
that I bear witness—
the cells on one hand,
the brain flying apart
on the other, a separation
comparable to the pulling apart
of continents, of galaxies.
And because I choose the cell
rather than the pistol,
I have lined up with all those
whom the government issue .45
is aimed at, a revolutionary
without politics
in line with my hands, my feet,
my heart; with my brain
that so easily flies apart:
in line with my brothers

and sisters
as we advance by twos
toward an ark still hidden
by mist and trees.

You will say this is simple,
too simple; that a man my age
should know that one cell
is often inferior to another;
that all cells are not equal;
that just as with bees,
there are worker cells
and management cells
and corporate board cells;
that the crowds of cells
were promised nothing,
have the right to nothing,
and can live comfortable,
decent lives on nothing.

But it's too late.
I've thrown in my lot
with the cells,
with their inalienable,
dignified movement,
their procession toward
all those inalienable things
brothers and sisters
want for their families.
I have chosen this
because the cell chooses
one direction over another,
just as the man behind the gun
chooses to pull the trigger.

Do you understand? Communist
has nothing to do with it.
Neither does Capitalist,
Fascist, or Democrat.
It is either the groping
brotherhood of the cell

or the oiled impact
crouching in the .45.

For this choice, each of us
bears witness for the other.

THE OTHER

- 1 -

It doesn't take long in this world
to realize that you're the other:
that the fried chicken and mashed potatoes,
arranged beside the buttered broccoli,
is a meal someone else won't eat;
that the GI blown apart in Asia,
bits of hair and intestine
plastered to the banyan leaves, isn't you,
and that the high school athlete paralyzed for life
isn't you, either. They're your brother
or your friend, cousin or acquaintance.
Maybe a stranger. Maybe.

But you are always the other,
the one who survives, who chews the chicken,
lopes into the end-zone, and dates the girl
he watched from across the street.
And when you fumble among her springing straps,
he is beside you, reaching out
like a breeze through the curtains,
circling your body and hers,
wrapping you both in a warm wind.

- 2 -

The coffee steams up from the white cup: nutty,
a chocolate sweetened with the rich, dark earth,
with all the dreams sighing in the rich, dark earth,
all the unaccomplished dreams of the dead.
You sip the coffee,
lumber through the tunnel of each day,
eat, dance, make love, imagining eyes that watch
from the road not taken, the tree not climbed,
the woman not loved,
the auto crash you did not die in.

And because even the strongest men
beat fists on their foreheads,
asking, "Why me? Why him? Why? Why?"
and only the wind answers, the wind
and the tall darkness;
because we begin and end
in that darkness—this life,
which we didn't want and never asked for,
is, at least for a time, as sort of answer;
is, for a time, a sort of reason;
is, right now, the only reason
to holler a greeting at the sun,
grab our loneliness with both hands
and waltz with it around the living room,
until our breath is gone and our heart aches
for love, for life, for all the dead.

I HAVE A TALK WITH MY RIGHT FOOT

You are supposed to be ticklish
but when touched remain impassive.
The tingling scurries through you
on its way to my giggling high above.
Remote, unresponsive, a shapeless shape,
you are the faithful servant
whose lips are forever shut.
And you are my servant—obedient,
self-effacing—who follows my directions
without complaint: just what I need
when launching the plump edges of my skin
into the winds and waves of other lives.

I must be sure of you, who lead the way:
there can be no stumblings. And so, lovingly,
I lock you up to keep you safe in dungeons
once the breathing sides of animals.
And all day you trudge those passages
in humid darkness, going no place
you can see or understand,
while outside and high above,
I laugh, holler, scream, and cry.

But I never forget you, do I?
Each night at this time, when I withdraw you
from your dungeon and hold you in both hands
as if you were a beautiful face,
don't I handle you tenderly
while gazing at your expressionless features?
It's true, we're not lovers,
but having shared so much
I think of us more as two companions
than as master and slave.

That's not much comfort, I know.
But I'll tell you this: there are moments
when I sense that I am nothing more
than an extension of you;

that my entire body is your leg.
At those instances of sorrow and joy,
of shrieky deliriums that shake
showers of needles in my nerve-ends,
I have recognized your dominance
and relinquished to you everything I am,
much as a small man allows the great dane
at the end of the leash to drag him
from street to street and into neighborhoods
where he would never go.

                                  And truth to tell,
I never feel freer than in those moments
when I bump along behind you in your rhythm,
as you stomp and pirouette on the pavement,
slap flat sole on floorboards or sand
in the only expression you can vent—
rage or celebration (I've never decided which):
rage or celebration, when you throw my arms
above my head and make me shout at the sky—
that dungeon which contains us all
and from which we'll never be released,
except maybe in those moments
of your dumb, numb dancing, Foot.

WHERE DO THE SHADOWS GO

Where do the shadows go:
the ones before noon and the ones after,
the shadows of the right and left sides?
Who packs them up and carts them away?

The boys, barechested and giggling,
found them in the old barn, sunlight
splintery through roof and rafters:
found them in the big space under the loft.

They were looking for something else, of course,
and when they found them they stacked them
against the wall like pairs of wings
they didn't understand and had no use for.

Shadows were places for old people
to sit in, or where their brothers
went with girls, so they chased each other
from the barn, forgetting where it was,

and when their parents asked, they rummaged
through the barn shadows in their heads
but couldn't remember. That day
a shadow passed over their lives:

they turned around and squinted.
The fields were the same in the sunlight
but somehow different. Beyond the fields
was the barn, but they didn't know where,

and at the edge of the field under the trees,
in ravines and ditches, a darkness was rising,
sharpening and changing and adding dimensions
to the flat light and naked hillsides.

From then on the boys had been obsessed
with where the shadows went. It was not a matter
of longing for the barn or the flat landscape,
but a twinge in their shoulder blades, a growing ache,

an awareness of wings that would eventually
enfold them in a smothering, forgetful sleep,
and whose absence on their shoulders
condemned them to trudge upon the ground.

SCULPTORS

Damn, but I admire sculptors:
They keep chipping away at the darkness
until it reveals a slender shoulder
rising completely unbruised from rock.
Wielding their mallets in one hand,
chisels in the other, they charge the void,
which towers above them as threatening
as an ocean wave, and demand it show itself
once and for all, always believing
there's a face or a starry crown
where we see nothing but stone.

Watch them stalk around the blank rock:
they squint and tilt their heads,
trying to glimpse the shape inside,
as if looking for a hiding child
who bites back its giggles
and holds its breath so it won't be found.

It's almost like a game of hide-and-seek,
as the sculptor taps on the window of stone
and the void refuses to let him in.
If the sculptor cannot gain entrance,
the void wins; and if he can,
he finds that the void has escaped
and the house is a shambles—
splinters of stone, pebbles, sand,
like a beach or a desert on a starless night.

This game is played in many ways:
an archaelogist, digging through layer
after layer of neuroses and guilt,
searches for a city buried within;
a prince hacks through a petrified wood
surrounding a castle clamped in ice
where Beauty waits for the chisel's kiss;
a parent or soldier limps toward a cave
at the end of the road, where a child,
strangling on vines, is about to be born.

So the sculptors pursue the changing features
that wash out to sea on the tides of sleep,
those primal features they can't quite recall
when they wake in the morning on familiar shores.
And as they peck at the expressionless mask,
probing for the contours they half-remember,
the void, clenched in its cradle of stone,
grips to itself in a death-like embrace
the memory of that unfathomable face.

THE POEM ABOUT LIGHT

- 1 -

The poem about light concerns

the glaze that sprawls
on the sunlit silver bells
in the tower two blocks over,
the glint from cars and bicycles
on the wineglasses near the window.

It concerns the sparklings
launched from bell to glass
and car to bike that pool
on platinum, pause on gold—

that liquid, languid, limpid light
that reclines on surfaces,
lolling on kettles,
cups, and knives.

- 2 -

This same light disappears
in crackers and dust, sinks

into the textured gaps
of paper, cotton, and wood.

It is the light
that falls through the window
into the faded orange carpet:

battalions of light, armies
of light, even angels of light—
all flowing hair and wings. It is

wheat fields in flame, a blond fire
streaming into the frowzy carpet.

- 3 -

The light falls past orange carpet fibers
and cigar ash and toenail clippings;

past bread crumbs and dust mites,
specks of dandruff and tobacco shreds.

It falls past two grains of sand
from the Great Pyramid and flakes—

no, more membranes than flakes—
that tremble when dogs bark across the street,

hum when footfalls sound in another room,
and toll when tapped by mandible and salt grain,

as if tiny gongs were vibrating
throughout the fibers of the carpet.

- 4 -

All this light caroming off bells, bounding
through windows, and borne by the wind

is nothing more than an exhalation,
an old man's last sigh before sleep,

a sigh that contains his whole life,
a history that sails into the evening

with billions of others—an armada
streaming past the frozen galaxies

like grains in a luminous ocean
sailing to the end of the universe.

But some grains slow, mired in eddies,
backwaters, stagnant coves of darkness,

and many are pulled back toward Earth,
and the light is pulled with them: filaments,

flashes, clusters of incandescent flakes
turning, surging backwards

and streaking down the sky—a boiling light
falling out of heaven, a steady rain

full of angel wings and flaming wheat,
pyramids and rhapsodic whisperings.

- 5 -

Every day radiant specks from this light
spatter the Earth, a constant shower
that pools and trembles, mirrors and bounds.
And every day we awaken
to the bells beyond the window,
and to the orange carpet in the living room
that for years we've meant to throw out.

OLD MEN, OLD WOMEN

You see them on park benches,
even in winter's gray light,
faces tilted skyward, eyes closed,
no longer enraged or ecstatic,
but draining a quiet contentment
from any warmth they can find.

Or they shuffle down the street,
placing each step with such care
that a stroll to the corner
becomes a tightrope walk
demanding a balance and precision
they are no longer sure of.

Old men, old women—they've learned
to be satisfied with winter's pale light,
new grass sprouting in the cracks
of pavement squares, and children
whose faces have been trapped for years
behind the glass of broken mirrors.

They remember mothers who warned them
to be good, to look both ways,
or someone older than time
would glare like their fathers and shout
down their years, but few can recall
the grandparents they have become.

Old men, old women: they sit, stroll, stare.
The sight of them dragging through our day,
stooping too long over the scrawniest weed
or loitering child, annoys us no end.
We want them to hurry, not celebrate
the ordinary as something miraculous—

like those pennies that blazed into gold
when we found them in our parents' pockets.
These old people, we want to forget them:

they remind us of the childhood
we walked away from and the decrepitude
we are so hurriedly striding toward.

But when we see them at street corners
we secretly watch as they wait
for the light to change, readying
their bodies like ships to launch
on the great adventure of crossing
to the park, as we did when young,

our parents' warnings in our ears
as their parents' must have been in theirs,
the first great voyage about to begin
when the world was new, as it is
each day to whoever undertakes
this journey we have forgotten.

CLEAR NIGHT

Twilight. Buses
open with a sigh.
Like book covers,
taxi doors
flop outward
and deposit us,
weary characters
from old novels,
at front doors.
Lights spring on
in house after house,
until the suburbs
sparkle. We steer
through familiar rooms
toward supper, talk,
and televison shows,
pulling curtains shut,
finally switching off
the lights we've lit
and dropping shoes
near beds we roll
ourselves into,
as, sighing, we turn
from yesterday
toward tomorrow,
sensing that we turn
in the huge dark
as the Earth does,
the stars revolving
in celestial suburbs
we may never understand
but have always lived in.

THE STARS

The stars are grains of salt
thrown over God's shoulder.
They fly from us and we fly after.

But the heart, that dark star,
the heart, that heavy planet,
is all we can know of heaven.

NO MATTER WHAT

No matter what I say,
this world will go on rushing
toward whatever worlds
rush toward, a blind eyeball
careening through cold depths
and scalding zones of heat.

The difference we make
is what we're supposed to make.
That makes no difference to me.
Whether anyone listens
or anyone hears, I'll say
whatever I need to say.

Like the white girl humming
on the bus, or the black kid
hollering a pop tune
as he dances down the street,
I'll sing simply to sing
and leave it at that.

And what I'll sing is praise
because that's what I need to do:
praise for the white girl on the bus
and the black kid on the street,
and praise for the eye
that sees nothing to praise

and praise for the nothing too.

SHOUTING DOWN THE SILENCE

When I lie down to sleep
and the hairs on my body stir,
somewhere, I'm sure of it, the trees
down the length of a mountain range
are fluttering in a moonlit breeze.
Not that this explains anything or restores
or even breaks the endless silence
of the broken pitcher lying on its side
in an abandoned shack, the rusty coat hangers
in empty lots, or any discarded thing,
nor that my mind will possibly invent a thought
that will change the contours of the universe
and show me a pathway through it,
but that at the moment of my death
I will be able to let my last breath go
with the same unthinking assurance
as that breeze sailing down the mountain range,
knowing that to every furred rib cage it ruffles,
and to every leaf and wing tip it nudges,
it murmurs in my voice, like a shout
down the silence, "I was here."

Photo by Jana Marcus

Morton Marcus is the author of eight volumes of poetry and one novel, among them *The Santa Cruz Mountain Poems*, *Pages From a Scrapbook of Immigrants*, and *When People Could Fly*. He has published over 400 poems in literary journals, and his work has appeared in more than 76 anthologies in the United States, Europe and Australia. His ninth book, *Moments Without Names: New & Selected Prose Poems*, was published earlier this year as part of the Marie Alexander Series of White Pine Press. In 1999, Marcus was named Santa Cruz County Artist of the Year, joining Adrienne Rich and William Everson (Brother Antoninus) as the only poets to win the award.